Going Fast

Written by Janice Vale

Contents

Collins

Going fast

Something that goes really fast often has a smooth, simple shape, and is strong and powerful. If something is **streamlined**, it will go faster as air will flow over it.

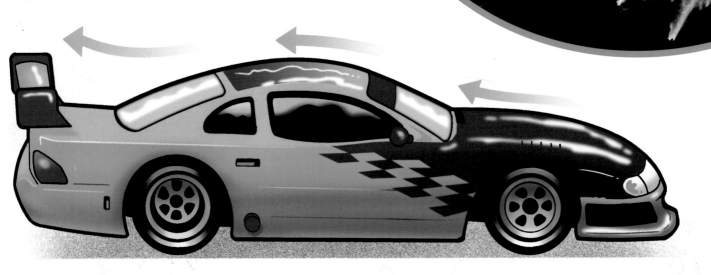

On land

Cheetahs are the fastest animals on land. They can run at 113 kilometres per hour. A cheetah has a small head, a long sleek body and powerful legs.

stretching

back arched
like a bow

back lowered
and head down

When a cheetah runs, it lowers its head,
stretches forward with its long legs and
bends its back.

A bobsleigh **hurtles** down a slope. It can go at 145 kilometres per hour. It has smooth steel runners and it slides down a smooth path of snow.

The team members push the bobsleigh across the ice to gather speed, then jump in as the bobsleigh crosses the start line.

Racing bikes are built to go fast. They have narrow wheels and light frames. The cyclist keeps his head down low, so that the air passes over him smoothly.

a streamlined helmet

the Easyrider motorbike

This motorbike goes as fast as 515 kilometres per hour. It doesn't look like a motorbike. It looks just like the nose of an aeroplane. This shape helps it to go very fast.

Here's a car that can race at 1,228 kilometres per hour – faster than the speed of sound. It has powerful jets to make it go this fast and parachutes to help stop it.

The "nose" of the Thrust SSR car is pointed to make it streamlined.

Concorde looked like a bird in the air.

On water

Dolphins have pointed **snouts** to help them move through the water. They have soft, flaky skin that they **shed** every two hours. This helps them to slide through the water quickly. Dolphins can go as fast as 40 kilometres per hour and they love to race against boats!

dolphins racing against a boat

17

a speedboat

a sailing boat

sailing boats

Boats are pointed at the **bow** to help them move through the water. Sailing boats need wind to blow them along. The bigger the sails, the faster the boats can go.

18

Here's one of the fastest boats to sail around the world. It is a trimaran. Most boats only have one **hull**, but this has three to make it go faster.

Speedboats have powerful motors at the **stern**. When they go really fast, the boat's bow lifts up, right out of the water.

This trimaran speeds through the water.

the boat's bow

Glossary

bow   the front of a boat

dive   drop headfirst towards the ground

hull   the main body of a boat

hurtles   goes very fast

shed   get rid of

snouts   animal noses

stern   the back of a boat

streamlined   a simple, smooth shape

supersonic   faster than the speed of sound

Index

A table

	cheetah	sleek body, powerful legs, lowers head
	bobsleigh	smooth steel runners, smooth path
	racing bike	light frame, cyclist keeps head down
	Easyrider motorbike	bike is covered, special shape
	Thrust SSR	low on the ground, powerful jets
	McLaren F1	low on the ground, powerful engines

	falcon	folds wings back, dives on prey
	Blackbird	special shape, powerful engine
	Concorde	nose like a bird, narrow shape, powerful engines
	dolphin	pointed snout, sheds skin
	sailing boat	pointed bow, large sails, uses wind for power
	speedboat	pointed bow, powerful engine at the stern

Ideas for guided reading

Learning objectives: explain ideas and processes using language and gesture appropriately; explain organisational features of texts, including alphabetical order, layout, diagrams, captions; explain their reactions to texts, commenting on important aspects; use syntax and context to self correct when reading for accuracy and meaning

Curriculum links: Science: Forces and movement

Interest words: bobsleigh, Concorde, falcon, McLaren F1, Thrust SSR, streamlined, supersonic

Resources: whiteboard, drawing materials

Word count: 454

Getting started

- Look at the covers and discuss possible answers to the questions in the blurb. Make a quick note of children's answers on the whiteboard.

- Read through pp2–3 together. Encourage the children to explain in their own words why a streamlined shape may travel faster. Return to the original questions about cheetahs and boats. Discuss if they are streamlined shapes.

- Leaf through the pages identifying and naming things that go fast.

- Introduce the interest words, modelling use of the glossary for the meaning of *supersonic*.

- Direct them to read one chapter in pairs, and answer the question: *What goes fast and why?*

Reading and responding

- Prompt and praise use of syntax and context to infer meaning.

- Early finishers read aloud to each other, using punctuation to help with expression.

- Ask the children to report what they have found out to the rest of the group using their own words to explain why things go fast.